Delicious
barbecue

Delicious

barbecue

Love Food ® is an imprint of Parragon Books Ltd

Parragon
Queen Street House
4 Queen Street
Bath BA1 1HE, UK

Copyright © Parragon Books Ltd 2008

Love Food ® and the accompanying heart device is a trademark of Parragon Books Ltd

Photography by Günter Beer
Home economy by Stevan Paul

ISBN 978-1-4075-3305-6

Printed in China

Notes for the reader
• This book uses imperial, metric, and US cup measurements. Follow the same units of measurement throughout; do not mix imperial and metric.
• All spoon measurements are level: teaspoons are assumed to be 5 ml, and tablespoons are assumed to be 15 ml.
• Unless otherwise stated, milk is assumed to be lowfat and eggs are medium. The times given are an approximate guide only.
• Some recipes contain nuts. If you are allergic to nuts you should avoid using them and any products containing nuts.
• Recipes using raw or very lightly cooked eggs should be avoided by infants, the elderly, pregnant women, convalescents, and anyone suffering from illness.

Contents

Introduction

If you mention summer cooking and entertaining to anyone, their first thought would have to be—barbecue! After the doom and gloom of cold wet winter days, the arrival of summer means a whole new way of cooking and eating. Barbecued food is easy to prepare, quick to cook, and the ideal sunshine food, and appeals to kids and adults alike. The allure of outdoor eating is not difficult to pinpoint—food tastes better in the fresh air and the delicious cooking smells only add to the hunger levels, which means food cooked outdoors is always well received! The recipes in this delightful collection will ensure your barbecue is a complete success, from stunning side dishes to marvelous mains.

One of the first things to consider when deciding to hold a barbecue is whether you want to use gas or charcoal for heat. This is more of a lifestyle choice. If you are convinced that food cooked over hot charcoal has the best flavor and take pride in getting the fire started, then charcoal is for you. Alternatively, if you want the perfect fire at the touch of a button and to be able to control the temperature, then a gas barbecue is the ideal choice.

If you opt for a charcoal barbecue, there are a few general rules you can follow to ensure success. Firstly, keep the charcoal briquettes dry, preferably in an airtight container, to help the charcoal light faster. Place the briquettes in a pyramid in the center of the grill. If you are using barbecue lighter fluid, douse this evenly over the briquettes and allow to soak in for a few minutes. If you are using barbecue fire lighters, poke these between the briquettes about a third of the way up the pyramid. Using long kitchen matches, light the doused briquettes or the

fire lighters. The charcoal will take about 30 minutes to get hot. Once the briquettes start to get hot, they will glow a red to orange color, then gradually turn to a whitish gray. It is the white ash over the coals that tells you they are really hot. Now you can spread them out evenly over the bottom of the barbecue. Do not worry if some of the coals from the center of the pyramid are still orange—just give them a few more minutes to turn gray too. Place the cooking metal grill over the top. It is a good idea to wait a few more minutes before adding the food, in order to allow the grill to heat up really well.

Barbecue food should be kept simple and fuss-free—without compromising on taste. The chapters in this book will cater for all tastes and will ensure your barbecue is a complete success. 'Meat & Poultry' contains all the classics no barbecue would be complete without, including a few new ideas – try the Brandied Steaks for a twist on the usual barbecued steaks. 'Fish & Seafood' provides mouthwatering ideas for delicious fish dishes, such as the Orange & Lemon Peppered Monkfish. Vegetarians are often forgotten about at barbecues or have to make do with a salad—try turning to the 'Vegetarian & Accompaniments' chapter for lots of exciting ideas that will please vegetarians and meat-lovers alike, such as the Zucchini & Cheese Packages. And to finish, 'Desserts & Treats' will provide plenty of sweet treats, such as the Toffee Fruit Kabobs. There is also a recipe for Sangria included—a nonalcoholic version, to avoid any barbecue mishaps!

So get the barbecue going and let this book guide you through the best barbecue food ever!

Meat & Poultry

serves 4

4 beef steaks

4 tbsp brandy or whiskey

2 tbsp soy sauce

1 tbsp dark brown sugar

2 large tomatoes, thickly
sliced

pepper

fresh flat-leaf parsley sprigs,
to garnish

garlic bread, to serve

brandied steaks

Make a few cuts in the edge of the fat on each steak. This will prevent the meat from curling as it cooks. Place the meat in a shallow, nonmetallic dish.

Mix the brandy, soy sauce, sugar, and pepper to taste together in a small bowl, stirring until the sugar dissolves. Pour the mixture over the steak. Cover with plastic wrap and let marinate in the refrigerator for at least 2 hours.

Preheat the barbecue. Cook the beef steaks over hot coals, searing the meat over the hottest part of the grill for 2 minutes on each side.

Move the meat to an area with slightly less intense heat and cook for an additional 4–10 minutes on each side, depending on how well done you like your steaks. To test if the meat is cooked, insert the point of a sharp knife into the meat—the juices will run from red when the meat is still rare, to clear as it becomes well cooked.

Lightly grill the tomato slices for 1–2 minutes. Transfer the meat and the tomatoes to serving plates. Garnish with fresh parsley sprigs and serve with garlic bread.

serves 4

2 tbsp corn oil, plus extra for oiling

finely grated rind of 1 lime

1 tbsp lime juice

2 garlic cloves, crushed

1/4 tsp ground coriander

1/4 tsp ground cumin

pinch of sugar

1 piece sirloin or top round, about 1 lb 8 oz/675 g and 3/4 inch/2 cm thick

4 flour tortillas

1 avocado

2 tomatoes, thinly sliced

4 tbsp sour cream

4 scallions, thinly sliced

salt and pepper

barbecued steak fajitas

To make the marinade, put the oil, lime rind and juice, garlic, coriander, cumin, sugar, and salt and pepper to taste into a large, shallow, nonmetallic dish that is large enough to hold the steak and mix together. Add the steak and turn in the marinade to coat it. Cover and let marinate in the refrigerator for 6–8 hours or up to 24 hours, turning occasionally.

When ready to cook, preheat the barbecue. Using a slotted spoon, remove the steak from the marinade, put onto the grill rack, and cook over medium heat for 5 minutes for rare or 8–10 minutes for medium, turning the steak frequently and basting once or twice with any remaining marinade.

Meanwhile, warm the tortillas according to the instructions on the package. Peel, pit, and slice the avocado.

Thinly slice the steak across the grain and arrange an equal quantity of the slices on one side of each tortilla. Add the tomato and avocado slices, top with a spoonful of sour cream, and sprinkle over the scallions. Fold over and eat immediately.

serves 4–6

1 lb/450 g sirloin or top round, freshly ground

1 onion, grated

2–4 garlic cloves, crushed

2 tsp whole grain mustard

2 tbsp olive oil

1 lb/450 g onions, finely sliced

2 tsp brown sugar

pepper

hamburger buns, to serve

the classic hamburger

Place the ground beef, grated onion, garlic, mustard, and pepper to taste in a large bowl and mix together. Shape into 4–6 equal-size burgers, then cover and let chill for 30 minutes.

Meanwhile, heat the oil in a heavy-bottom skillet. Add the finely sliced onions and cook over low heat for 10–15 minutes, or until the onions have caramelized. Add the sugar after 8 minutes and stir occasionally during cooking. Drain well on paper towels and keep warm.

Preheat the barbecue. Cook the burgers over hot coals for 3–5 minutes on each side or until cooked to personal preference. Serve in hamburger buns with the onions.

serves 2

8 oz/225 g beef tenderloin,
about 1 inch/2.5 cm thick

8 raw jumbo shrimp,
in their shells

olive oil, for oiling

4 tbsp butter

2 garlic cloves, crushed

3 tbsp chopped fresh flat-leaf
parsley, plus extra sprigs
to garnish

finely grated rind and juice of
1 lime

salt and pepper

lime wedges, to garnish

crusty bread, to serve

surf & turf skewers

Cut the steak into 1-inch/2.5-cm cubes. To prepare the shrimp, pull off their heads with your fingers, then peel off their shells. Using a sharp knife, make a shallow slit along the back of each shrimp, then pull out the dark vein and discard. Rinse the shrimp under cold running water and dry well on paper towels.

Thread an equal number of the steak cubes and shrimp onto 2 oiled metal kabob skewers or presoaked wooden skewers. Season the kabobs to taste with pepper.

Preheat the barbecue. Meanwhile, put the butter and garlic into a small pan and heat gently until melted. Remove from the heat and add the chopped parsley, lime rind and juice, and salt and pepper to taste. Leave in a warm place so that the butter remains melted.

Brush the kabobs with a little of the melted butter. Put the kabobs onto an oiled grill rack and cook over medium heat for 4–8 minutes until the steak is cooked according to your taste and the shrimp turn pink, turning the kabobs frequently during cooking, and brushing with some of the remaining melted butter.

Serve the kabobs hot on the skewers, with the remaining butter spooned over. Garnish with lime wedges and parsley sprigs and serve with crusty bread to mop up the buttery juices.

serves 4

4 lean pork loin chops

4 tbsp clear honey

1 tbsp dry sherry

4 tbsp orange juice

2 tbsp olive oil

1-inch/2.5-cm piece
fresh ginger, grated

corn oil, for oiling

salt and pepper

honey-glazed pork chops

Preheat the barbecue. Season the pork chops with salt and pepper to taste. Reserve while you make the glaze.

To make the glaze, place the honey, sherry, orange juice, olive oil, and ginger in a small pan and heat gently, stirring constantly, until well blended.

Cook the pork chops on an oiled rack over hot coals for 5 minutes on each side.

Brush the chops with the glaze and cook for an additional 2–4 minutes on each side, basting frequently with the glaze.

Transfer the pork chops to warmed serving plates and serve hot.

serves 4

1 onion, chopped

2 garlic cloves, chopped

1-inch/2.5-cm piece
fresh ginger, sliced

1 fresh red chile, seeded and
chopped

5 tbsp dark soy sauce

3 tbsp lime juice

1 tbsp brown sugar

2 tbsp peanut oil

2 lb 4 oz/1 kg pork spareribs,
separated

salt and pepper

fresh cilantro sprigs,
to garnish

spicy ribs

Preheat the barbecue. Put the onion, garlic, ginger, chile, and soy sauce into a food processor and process to a paste. Transfer to a measuring cup and stir in the lime juice, sugar, and oil. Season to taste with salt and pepper.

Place the spareribs in a preheated wok or large, heavy-bottom pan and pour in the soy sauce mixture. Place on the stove and bring to a boil, then let simmer over low heat, stirring frequently, for 30 minutes. If the mixture appears to be drying out, add a little water.

Remove the spareribs, reserving the sauce. Cook the ribs over medium–hot coals, turning and basting frequently with the sauce, for 20–30 minutes. Transfer to a large serving plate and serve immediately, garnished with cilantro sprigs.

serves 4

1 lb/450 g pork fillet

1¹/4 cups hard cider

1 tbsp chopped fresh sage

6 black peppercorns, crushed

2 crisp apples

1 tbsp corn oil

crusty bread, to serve

pork & apple brochettes

Using a sharp knife, cut the pork into 1-inch/2.5-cm cubes, then place in a large, shallow, nonmetallic dish. Mix the cider, sage, and peppercorns together in a measuring cup, pour the mixture over the pork, and turn until thoroughly coated. Cover and let marinate in the refrigerator for 1–2 hours.

Preheat the barbecue. Drain the pork, reserving the marinade. Core the apples, but do not peel, then cut into wedges. Dip the apple wedges into the marinade and thread onto several metal skewers, alternating with the cubes of pork. Stir the corn oil into the remaining marinade.

Cook the brochettes over medium–hot coals, turning and brushing frequently with the reserved marinade, for 12–15 minutes. Transfer to a large serving plate and, if you prefer, remove the meat and apples from the skewers before serving. Serve immediately with crusty bread.

serves 6

6 lamb chops, about
6 oz/175 g each

2/3 cup strained plain yogurt

2 garlic cloves, finely
chopped

1 tsp grated fresh ginger

1/4 tsp coriander seeds,
crushed

1 tbsp olive oil, plus extra for
brushing

1 tbsp orange juice

1 tsp walnut oil

2 tbsp chopped fresh mint,
plus sprigs to garnish

salt and pepper

minted lamb chops

Place the chops in a large, shallow, nonmetallic bowl. Mix half the yogurt, the garlic, ginger, and coriander seeds together in a measuring cup and season to taste with salt and pepper. Spoon the mixture over the chops, turning to coat, then cover with plastic wrap and let marinate in the refrigerator for 2 hours, turning occasionally.

Preheat the barbecue. Place the remaining yogurt, the olive oil, orange juice, walnut oil, and chopped mint in a small bowl and, using a handheld blender, mix until thoroughly blended. Season to taste with salt and pepper. Cover the minted yogurt with plastic wrap and let chill in the refrigerator until ready to serve.

Drain the chops, scraping off the marinade. Brush with olive oil and cook over medium–hot coals for 5–7 minutes on each side. Garnish with mint sprigs and serve immediately with the minted yogurt.

serves 4

4 chicken drumsticks

4 chicken thighs

2 fresh corn cobs, husks and
silks removed

3 oz/85 g butter, melted

fresh flat-leaf parsley sprigs,
to garnish

spice mix

2 tsp onion powder

2 tsp paprika

1½ tsp salt

1 tsp garlic powder

1 tsp dried thyme

1 tsp cayenne pepper

1 tsp ground black pepper

½ tsp ground white pepper

¼ tsp ground cumin

cajun chicken

Preheat the barbecue. Using a sharp knife, make 2–3 diagonal slashes in the chicken drumsticks and thighs, then place them in a large dish. Cut the corn cobs into thick slices and add them to the dish. Mix all the ingredients for the spice mix together in a small bowl.

Brush the chicken and corn with the melted butter and sprinkle with the spice mix. Toss to coat well.

Cook the chicken over medium–hot coals, turning occasionally, for 15 minutes, then add the corn slices and cook, turning occasionally, for an additional 10–15 minutes, or until starting to blacken slightly at the edges. Transfer to a large serving plate and serve immediately.

serves 4

4 lean chicken parts

1 bunch scallions, trimmed

1–2 chiles (Scotch bonnet, if possible)

1 garlic clove

2-inch/5-cm piece fresh ginger, coarsely chopped

1/2 tsp dried thyme

1/2 tsp paprika

1/4 tsp ground allspice

pinch of ground cinnamon

pinch of ground cloves

4 tbsp white wine vinegar

3 tbsp light soy sauce

pepper

jerk chicken

Rinse the chicken parts and pat them dry on paper towels. Place them in a shallow dish.

Place the scallions, chiles, garlic, ginger, thyme, paprika, allspice, cinnamon, cloves, vinegar, soy sauce, and pepper to taste in a food processor and process until smooth.

Pour the spicy mixture over the chicken. Turn the chicken parts over so that they are well coated in the marinade.

Transfer the chicken parts to the refrigerator and leave to marinate for up to 24 hours.

Remove the chicken from the marinade and grill over medium–hot coals for about 30 minutes, turning the chicken over and basting occasionally with any remaining marinade, until the chicken is browned and cooked through.

Transfer the chicken parts to individual serving plates and serve immediately.

serves 4

4 large chicken breast fillets, skinned

1 large egg white

1 tbsp cornstarch

1 tbsp all-purpose flour

1 egg, beaten

1 cup fresh white breadcrumbs

2 tbsp corn oil

2 beefsteak tomatoes, sliced

to serve

hamburger buns

lettuce

mayonnaise

the ultimate chicken burger

Place the chicken breasts between 2 sheets of nonstick parchment paper and flatten slightly using a meat mallet or a rolling pin. Beat the egg white and cornstarch together, then brush over the chicken. Cover and let chill for 30 minutes, then coat in the flour.

Place the egg and breadcrumbs in 2 separate bowls and coat the burgers first in the egg, allowing any excess to drip back into the bowl, then in the breadcrumbs.

Preheat the barbecue. When hot, add the burgers and cook over hot coals for 6–8 minutes on each side, or until thoroughly cooked. If you are in doubt, it is worth cutting one of the burgers in half. If there is any sign of pinkness, cook for a little longer. Add the tomato slices for the last 1–2 minutes of the cooking time to heat through. Serve the burgers in hamburger buns with the lettuce, cooked tomato slices, and mayonnaise.

serves 4

4 skinless, boneless chicken breasts, about 6 oz/175 g each

finely grated rind and juice of 1/2 lemon

finely grated rind and juice of 1/2 orange

2 tbsp honey

2 tbsp olive oil

2 tbsp chopped fresh mint, plus extra to garnish

1/4 tsp ground coriander

salt and pepper

citrus zest, to garnish

zesty kabobs

Using a sharp knife, cut the chicken into 1-inch/2.5-cm cubes, then place them in a large glass bowl. Place the lemon and orange rind, the lemon and orange juice, the honey, oil, mint, and ground coriander in a measuring cup and mix together. Season to taste with salt and pepper. Pour the marinade over the chicken cubes and toss until thoroughly coated. Cover with plastic wrap and let marinate in the refrigerator for up to 8 hours.

Preheat the barbecue. Drain the chicken cubes, reserving the marinade. Thread the chicken onto several long metal skewers.

Cook the skewers over medium–hot coals, turning and brushing frequently with the reserved marinade, for 6–10 minutes, or until thoroughly cooked. Transfer to a large serving plate, garnish with chopped mint and citrus zest, and serve immediately.

Fish & Seafood

serves 4

4 salmon steaks, about
6 oz/175 g each

finely grated rind
and juice of 1 lime or
1/2 lemon

salt and pepper

mango salsa

1 large mango, peeled, pitted,
and diced

1 red onion, finely chopped

2 passion fruit

2 fresh basil sprigs

2 tbsp lime juice

salt

salmon with mango salsa

Preheat the barbecue. Rinse the salmon steaks under cold running water, pat dry with paper towels, and place in a large, shallow, nonmetallic dish. Sprinkle with the lime rind and pour the juice over them. Season to taste with salt and pepper, cover, and let stand while you make the salsa.

To make the salsa, place the mango flesh in a bowl with the onion. Cut the passion fruit in half and scoop out the seeds and pulp with a teaspoon into the bowl. Tear the basil leaves and add them to the bowl with the lime juice. Season to taste with salt and stir. Cover with plastic wrap and set aside until required.

Cook the salmon steaks over medium–hot coals for 3–4 minutes on each side. Serve immediately with the salsa.

serves 4

4 whitefish steaks

1 tbsp paprika

1 tsp dried thyme

1 tsp cayenne pepper

1 tsp black pepper

1/2 tsp white pepper

1/2 tsp salt

1/4 tsp ground allspice

1 3/4 oz/50 g unsalted butter

3 tbsp corn oil

green beans, to serve

charred fish

Preheat the barbecue. Rinse the fish steaks under cold running water and pat dry with paper towels.

Mix the paprika, thyme, cayenne, black and white peppers, salt, and ground allspice together in a shallow dish.

Place the butter and corn oil in a small pan and heat gently, stirring occasionally, until the butter melts.

Brush the butter mixture liberally all over the fish steaks, on both sides, then dip the fish into the spicy mixture until coated on both sides.

Cook the fish over hot coals for 5 minutes on each side until cooked through. Continue to baste the fish with the remaining butter mixture during the cooking time. Serve with the green beans.

serves 4

4 tuna steaks, about
6 oz/175 g each

grated rind and juice
of 1 lime

2 tbsp olive oil

salt and pepper

fresh cilantro sprigs,
to garnish

lettuce leaves and crusty
bread, to serve

chile sauce

2 orange bell peppers

1 tbsp olive oil

juice of 1 lime

juice of 1 orange

2–3 fresh red chiles, seeded
and chopped

pinch of cayenne pepper

chargrilled tuna with chile sauce

Rinse the tuna thoroughly under cold running water and pat dry with paper towels, then place in a large, shallow, nonmetallic dish. Sprinkle with the lime rind and pour the juice and oil over the fish. Season to taste with salt and pepper, cover with plastic wrap, and let marinate in the refrigerator for up to 1 hour.

Preheat the barbecue. To make the sauce, brush the bell peppers with the oil and cook over hot coals, turning frequently, for 10 minutes, or until the skin is blackened and charred. Remove from the barbecue and let cool slightly, then remove the skins and discard the seeds. Put the bell peppers into a food processor with the remaining sauce ingredients and process to a puree. Transfer to a bowl and season to taste with salt and pepper.

Cook the tuna over hot coals for 4–5 minutes on each side, until golden. Transfer to serving plates, garnish with cilantro sprigs, and serve with the chile sauce, lettuce leaves, and plenty of crusty bread.

serves 4–6

8 oz/225 g sweet potatoes, chopped

1 lb/450 g fresh tuna steaks

6 scallions, finely chopped

6 oz/175 g zucchini, grated

1 fresh red jalapeño chile, seeded and finely chopped

2 tbsp prepared mango chutney

1 tbsp corn oil

salt

lettuce leaves, to serve

mango salsa

1 large ripe mango, peeled and pitted

2 ripe tomatoes, finely chopped

1 fresh red jalapeño chile, seeded and finely chopped

1½-inch/4-cm piece cucumber, finely diced

1 tbsp chopped fresh cilantro

1–2 tsp honey

tuna burgers with mango salsa

Cook the sweet potatoes in a pan of lightly salted boiling water for 15–20 minutes, or until tender. Drain well, then mash and place in a food processor. Cut the tuna into chunks and add to the potatoes.

Add the scallions, zucchini, chile, and mango chutney to the food processor and, using the pulse button, blend together. Shape into 4–6 equal-size burgers, then cover and let chill for 1 hour.

Meanwhile, make the salsa. Slice the mango flesh, reserving 8–12 good slices for serving. Finely chop the remainder, then mix with the tomatoes, chile, cucumber, cilantro, and honey. Mix well, then spoon into a small bowl. Cover and let stand for 30 minutes to allow the flavors to develop.

Preheat the barbecue. Brush the burgers lightly with oil and cook over hot coals for 4–6 minutes on each side, or until piping hot. Serve with the mango salsa, and garnish with lettuce leaves and the reserved slices of mango.

serves 4

1 lb 7 oz/650 g raw jumbo shrimp

6 scallions

1¾ cups coconut milk

finely grated rind and juice of 1 lime

4 tbsp chopped fresh cilantro, plus extra to garnish

2 tbsp corn oil

pepper

lemon wedges, to garnish

coconut shrimp

To prepare the shrimp, pull off their heads with your fingers, then peel off their shells. Using a sharp knife, make a shallow slit along the back of each shrimp, then pull out the dark vein and discard. Rinse the shrimp under cold running water and dry well on paper towels.

Finely chop the scallions and place in a large, shallow, nonmetallic dish with the coconut milk, lime rind and juice, cilantro, and oil. Mix well and season to taste with pepper. Add the shrimp, turning to coat. Cover with plastic wrap and let marinate in the refrigerator for 1 hour.

Preheat the barbecue. Drain the shrimp, reserving the marinade. Thread the shrimp onto 8 long metal skewers.

Cook the skewers over medium–hot coals, brushing with the reserved marinade and turning frequently, for 8 minutes, or until they have changed color. Serve the shrimp immediately, garnished with the lemon wedges and chopped cilantro.

serves 6

36 raw jumbo shrimp

2 tbsp finely chopped fresh
cilantro

pinch of cayenne pepper

3–4 tbsp corn oil

fresh cilantro leaves,
to garnish

lemon wedges, to serve

sauce

1 orange

1 tart apple, peeled,
quartered, and cored

2 fresh red chiles,
seeded and chopped

1 garlic clove, chopped

8 fresh cilantro sprigs

8 fresh mint sprigs

4 tbsp lime juice

salt and pepper

shrimp with citrus sauce

Preheat the barbecue. To make the sauce, peel the orange and cut into segments. Set aside any juice. Put the orange segments, apple quarters, chiles, garlic, cilantro, and mint into a food processor and process until smooth. With the motor running, add the lime juice through the feeder tube. Transfer the sauce to a serving bowl and season to taste with salt and pepper. Cover with plastic wrap and let chill in the refrigerator until required.

Using a sharp knife, make a shallow slit along the back of each shrimp, then pull out the dark vein and discard. Rinse the shrimp under cold running water and dry well on paper towels. Mix the chopped cilantro, cayenne, and corn oil together in a dish. Add the shrimp and toss well to coat.

Cook the shrimp over medium–hot coals for 3 minutes on each side, or until they have changed color. Transfer to a large serving plate, garnish with fresh cilantro leaves, and serve immediately with lemon wedges and the sauce.

serves 8

2 oranges

2 lemons

2 monkfish tails, about
1 lb 2 oz/500 g each, skinned
and cut into 4 fillets

8 fresh lemon thyme sprigs

2 tbsp olive oil

2 tbsp green peppercorns,
lightly crushed

salt

orange & lemon peppered monkfish

Cut 8 orange slices and 8 lemon slices, reserving the remaining fruit. Rinse the monkfish fillets under cold running water and pat dry with paper towels. Place the monkfish fillets, cut side up, on a counter and divide the citrus slices among them. Top with the lemon thyme. Tie each fillet at intervals with kitchen string to secure the citrus slices and thyme. Place the monkfish in a large, shallow, nonmetallic dish.

Squeeze the juice from the remaining fruit and mix with the oil in a measuring cup. Season to taste with salt, then spoon the mixture over the fish. Cover with plastic wrap and let marinate in the refrigerator for up to 1 hour, spooning the marinade over the fish once or twice.

Preheat the barbecue. Drain the monkfish, reserving the marinade. Sprinkle the crushed green peppercorns over the fish, pressing them in with your fingers. Cook the monkfish over medium–hot coals, turning and brushing frequently with the reserved marinade, for 20–25 minutes. Transfer to a cutting board, remove and discard the string, and cut the monkfish into slices. Serve immediately.

serves 6

2 lb 4 oz/1 kg swordfish
steaks

3 tbsp olive oil

3 tbsp lime juice

1 garlic clove, finely chopped

1 tsp paprika

3 onions, cut into wedges

6 tomatoes, cut into wedges

salt and pepper

caribbean fish kabobs

Using a sharp knife, cut the fish into 1-inch/2.5-cm cubes and place in a shallow, nonmetallic dish. Place the oil, lime juice, garlic, and paprika in a measuring cup and mix. Season to taste with salt and pepper. Pour the marinade over the fish, turning to coat. Cover with plastic wrap and let marinate in the refrigerator for 1 hour.

Preheat the barbecue. Thread the fish cubes, onion, and tomato wedges alternately onto 6 long, presoaked wooden skewers. Set aside the marinade.

Cook the kabobs over medium–hot coals for 8–10 minutes, turning and brushing frequently with the reserved marinade. When they are cooked through, transfer the kabobs to a large serving plate and serve immediately.

serves 6

36 fresh oysters

18 rindless lean bacon strips

1 tbsp mild paprika

1 tsp cayenne pepper

sauce

1 fresh red chile, seeded and finely chopped

1 garlic clove, finely chopped

1 shallot, finely chopped

2 tbsp finely chopped fresh parsley

2 tbsp lemon juice

salt and pepper

chargrilled devils

Preheat the barbecue. Open the oysters, catching the juice from the shells in a bowl. Cut the oysters from the bottom shells, set aside, and tip any remaining juice into the bowl. To make the sauce, add the chile, garlic, shallot, parsley, and lemon juice to the bowl, then season to taste with salt and pepper and mix well. Cover the bowl with plastic wrap and let chill in the refrigerator until required.

Using a sharp knife, cut each bacon strip in half across the center. Season the oysters with paprika and cayenne, then roll each oyster up inside half a bacon strip. Thread 6 wrapped oysters onto each presoaked wooden skewer.

Cook over hot coals, turning frequently, for 5 minutes, or until the bacon is well browned and crispy. Transfer to a large serving plate and serve immediately with the sauce.

Vegetarian & Accompaniments

serves 4–6

scant 1/2 cup brown rice

14 oz/400 g canned flageolets, drained

scant 1 cup unsalted cashews

3 garlic cloves

1 red onion, cut into wedges

1/2 cup corn kernels

2 tbsp tomato paste

1 tbsp chopped fresh oregano

2 tbsp whole wheat flour

2 tbsp corn oil

salt and pepper

to serve

hamburger buns

lettuce leaves

tomato slices

cheese slices

the ultimate vegetarian burger

Cook the rice in a pan of lightly salted boiling water for 20 minutes, or until tender. Drain and place in a food processor.

Add the beans, cashews, garlic, onion, corn, tomato paste, oregano, and salt and pepper to taste to the rice in the food processor and, using the pulse button, blend together. Shape into 4–6 equal-size burgers, then coat in the flour. Cover and let chill for 1 hour.

Preheat the barbecue. Brush the burgers lightly with oil and cook over hot coals for 5–6 minutes on each side or until cooked and piping hot. Serve the burgers in hamburger buns with the lettuce leaves, and tomato and cheese slices.

serves 4

12 oz/350 g firm tofu

1 red bell pepper

1 yellow bell pepper

2 zucchini

8 button mushrooms

shredded carrot and lemon
wedges, to garnish

marinade

grated rind and
juice of 1/2 lemon

1 garlic clove, crushed

1/2 tsp chopped fresh
rosemary

1/2 tsp chopped fresh thyme

1 tbsp walnut oil

marinated tofu skewers

To make the marinade, mix the lemon rind and juice, garlic, rosemary, thyme, and walnut oil together in a shallow dish. Drain the tofu, pat it dry on paper towels, and cut it into squares. Add to the marinade and toss to coat. Let marinate for 20–30 minutes.

Preheat the barbecue. Seed the bell peppers and cut into 1-inch/2.5-cm pieces. Blanch in boiling water for 4 minutes, refresh in cold water, and drain. Using a channel knife or potato peeler, remove strips of peel from the zucchini. Cut the zucchini into 1-inch/2.5-cm chunks.

Remove the tofu from the marinade, reserving the liquid for basting. Thread the tofu onto 8 presoaked wooden skewers, alternating with the bell peppers, zucchini, and mushrooms.

Cook the skewers over medium–hot coals for 6 minutes, turning and basting with the marinade. Transfer the skewers to warmed serving plates, garnish with shredded carrot and lemon wedges, and serve.

serves 2

2 large zucchini

1 tbsp olive oil, plus extra for brushing

4 oz/115 g feta cheese, cut into strips

1 tbsp chopped fresh mint

pepper

zucchini & cheese packages

Preheat the barbecue. Cut out 2 rectangles of foil, each large enough to enclose a zucchini, and brush lightly with oil. Cut a few slits along the length of each zucchini and place them on the foil rectangles.

Insert strips of feta cheese along the slits in the zucchini, then drizzle the olive oil over the top, sprinkle with mint, and season to taste with pepper. Fold in the sides of the foil rectangles securely and seal the edges to enclose the cheese-filled zucchini completely.

Bake the packages in the barbecue embers for 30–40 minutes. Carefully unwrap the packages and serve immediately.

serves 4

1 tbsp olive oil

2 tbsp pine nuts

1 onion, finely chopped

1 garlic clove, finely chopped

1 lb 2 oz/500 g fresh spinach, thick stalks removed and leaves shredded

pinch of freshly grated nutmeg

4 beefsteak tomatoes

5 oz/140 g mozzarella cheese, diced

salt and pepper

stuffed tomato packages

Preheat the barbecue. Heat the oil in a heavy-bottom pan. Add the pine nuts and cook, stirring constantly, for 2 minutes, or until golden. Add the onion and cook over low heat, stirring occasionally, for 5 minutes, or until softened but not browned. Add the garlic and spinach, cover, and cook for 2–3 minutes, or until the spinach has wilted. Remove the pan from the heat and season to taste with nutmeg, salt, and pepper. Let cool.

Using a sharp knife, cut off and set aside a thin slice from the top of each tomato and scoop out the flesh with a teaspoon, taking care not to pierce the shell. Chop the flesh and stir it into the spinach mixture with the mozzarella cheese.

Fill the tomato shells with the spinach and cheese mixture and replace the tops. Cut 4 squares of foil, each large enough to enclose a tomato. Place one tomato in the center of each square and fold up the sides to enclose securely. Cook over hot coals, turning occasionally, for 10 minutes. Serve immediately in the foil packages.

serves 12

12 portobello mushrooms

4 tsp olive oil

4 scallions, chopped

2 cups fresh brown breadcrumbs

1 tsp chopped fresh oregano

3½ oz/100 g feta cheese, crumbled

corn oil, for oiling

stuffed mushrooms

Preheat the barbecue. Remove the stems from the mushrooms and chop the stems finely. Heat half of the oil in a large skillet. Add the mushroom stems and scallions and cook briefly.

Mix the mushroom stems and scallions together in a large bowl. Add the breadcrumbs and oregano, mix well, then reserve until required.

Add the feta cheese to the breadcrumb mixture and mix well. Spoon the stuffing mixture into the mushroom caps.

Drizzle the remaining oil over the stuffed mushrooms, then cook on an oiled rack over medium–hot coals for 8–10 minutes. Transfer the mushrooms to individual serving plates and serve while still hot.

serves 4

1 red onion

1 fennel bulb

4 baby eggplants

4 baby zucchini

1 orange bell pepper

1 red bell pepper

2 beefsteak tomatoes

2 tbsp olive oil

salt and pepper

1 fresh basil sprig,
to garnish

creamy pesto

4 tbsp fresh basil leaves

1 tbsp pine nuts

1 garlic clove

pinch of coarse sea salt

1/4 cup freshly grated
Parmesan cheese

1/4 cup extra virgin
olive oil

2/3 cup strained plain yogurt

charbroiled vegetables with creamy pesto

Preheat the barbecue. To make the creamy pesto, place the basil, pine nuts, garlic, and sea salt in a mortar and pound to a paste with a pestle. Gradually work in the Parmesan cheese, then gradually stir in the oil.

Place the yogurt in a small serving bowl and stir in 3–4 tablespoons of the pesto mixture. Cover with plastic wrap and let chill in the refrigerator until required. Store any leftover pesto mixture in a screw-top jar in the refrigerator.

Prepare the vegetables. Cut the onion and fennel bulb into wedges, trim and slice the eggplants and zucchini, seed and thickly slice the bell peppers, and cut the tomatoes in half. Brush the vegetables with oil and season to taste with salt and pepper.

Cook the eggplants and bell peppers over hot coals for 3 minutes, then add the zucchini, onion, fennel, and tomatoes and cook, turning occasionally and brushing with more oil if necessary, for an additional 5 minutes. Transfer to a large serving plate and serve with the pesto, garnished with a basil sprig.

serves 4

8 oz/225 g dried fusilli

4 tomatoes

scant 1/3 cup black olives

1 oz/25 g sun-dried tomatoes
in oil

2 tbsp pine nuts

2 tbsp freshly grated
Parmesan cheese

salt

fresh basil leaves,
to garnish

vinaigrette

1/2 oz/15 g basil leaves

1 garlic clove, crushed

2 tbsp freshly grated
Parmesan cheese

4 tbsp extra virgin olive oil

2 tbsp lemon juice

salt and pepper

pasta salad with basil vinaigrette

Cook the pasta in a large pan of lightly salted boiling water for 10–12 minutes, or until just tender but still firm to the bite. Drain the pasta, rinse under cold running water, then drain again thoroughly. Place the pasta in a large bowl.

Preheat the broiler to medium. To make the vinaigrette, place the basil leaves, garlic, cheese, oil, and lemon juice in a food processor. Season to taste with salt and pepper and process until the leaves are well chopped and the ingredients are combined. Alternatively, finely chop the basil leaves by hand and combine with the other vinaigrette ingredients. Pour the vinaigrette over the pasta and toss to coat.

Cut the tomatoes into wedges. Pit and halve the olives. Slice the sun-dried tomatoes. Toast the pine nuts on a cookie sheet under the hot broiler until golden.

Add the tomatoes (fresh and sun-dried) and the olives to the pasta and mix until combined.

Transfer the pasta to a serving dish, sprinkle over the Parmesan and toasted pine nuts, and serve garnished with a few basil leaves.

serves 4

12 oz/350 g green beans, trimmed

1 red onion, chopped

3–4 tbsp chopped fresh cilantro

2 radishes, thinly sliced

3/4 cup crumbled feta cheese

1 tsp chopped fresh oregano or 1/2 tsp dried oregano

2 tbsp red wine vinegar or fruit vinegar

5 tbsp extra virgin olive oil

6 ripe cherry tomatoes, quartered

pepper

green bean & feta salad

Bring about 2 inches/5 cm of water to a boil in the bottom of a steamer or in a medium saucepan. Add the green beans to the top of the steamer or place them in a metal colander set over the pan of water. Cover and steam for about 5 minutes until just tender.

Transfer the beans to a bowl and add the onion, cilantro, radishes, and feta cheese.

Sprinkle the oregano over the salad, then season to taste with pepper. Whisk the vinegar and oil together and then pour over the salad. Toss gently to mix well.

Transfer to a serving platter, surround with the tomato quarters, and serve immediately or chill until ready to serve.

serves 4

1 lb 9 oz/700 g tiny new potatoes

8 scallions

1 hard-cooked egg (optional)

1 cup mayonnaise

1 tsp paprika, plus extra to garnish

salt and pepper

2 tbsp snipped fresh chives, to garnish

potato salad

Bring a large pan of lightly salted water to a boil. Add the potatoes and cook for 10–15 minutes, or until just tender.

Drain the potatoes and rinse them under cold running water until completely cold. Drain again. Transfer the potatoes to a bowl and reserve until required. Using a sharp knife, slice the scallions thinly on the diagonal. Chop the hard-cooked egg, if using.

Mix the mayonnaise, paprika, and salt and pepper to taste together in a bowl. Pour the mixture over the potatoes. Add the scallions and egg, if using, to the potatoes and toss together.

Transfer the potato salad to a serving bowl and sprinkle with snipped chives and a pinch of paprika. Cover and let chill in the refrigerator until required.

serves 4–6

8 small baking potatoes,
scrubbed

1³/4 oz/50 g butter, melted

salt and pepper

optional topping

6 scallions, sliced

¹/2 cup grated Gruyère cheese

crispy potato skins

Preheat the oven to 400°F/200°C. Prick the potatoes with a fork and bake in the preheated oven for 1 hour, or until tender. Alternatively, cook in a microwave on High for 12–15 minutes. Cut the potatoes in half and scoop out the flesh, leaving about ¹/4 inch/5 mm potato flesh lining the skin.

Preheat the barbecue. Brush the insides of the potatoes with melted butter.

Place the skins, cut-side down, over medium–hot coals and cook for 10–15 minutes. Turn the potato skins over and cook for an additional 5 minutes, or until they are crispy. Take care that they do not burn. Season the potato skins with salt and pepper to taste and serve while they are still warm.

If desired, the skins can be filled with a variety of toppings. Grill the potato skins as above for 10 minutes, then turn cut-side up and sprinkle with the scallions and Gruyère cheese. Cook for an additional 5 minutes, or until the cheese begins to melt. Serve hot.

serves 6

5¹/2 oz/150 g butter, softened

3 garlic cloves, crushed

2 tbsp chopped fresh parsley

1 large or 2 small loaves of
French bread

pepper

garlic bread

Mix together the butter, garlic, and parsley in a bowl until well combined. Season with pepper to taste and mix well.

Cut a few lengthways slits in the French bread. Spread the flavored butter inside the slits and place the bread on a large sheet of thick aluminum foil.

Preheat the barbecue. Wrap the bread well in the foil and cook over hot coals for 10–15 minutes, until the butter melts and the bread is piping hot.

Serve as an accompaniment to a wide range of dishes.

Desserts & Treats

serves 4

2 apples, cored and cut into wedges

2 firm pears, cored and cut into wedges

juice of $1/2$ lemon

2 tbsp brown sugar

$1/4$ tsp ground allspice

1 oz/25 g unsalted butter, melted

toffee sauce

$4^1/2$ oz/125 g butter

$1/2$ cup brown sugar

6 tbsp heavy cream

toffee fruit kabobs

Preheat the barbecue. Toss the apples and pears in the lemon juice to prevent any discoloration.

Mix the sugar and allspice together and sprinkle over the fruit. Thread the fruit pieces onto skewers.

To make the sauce, place the butter and sugar in a pan and heat, stirring gently, until the butter has melted and the sugar has dissolved. Add the cream to the pan and bring to a boil. Boil for 1–2 minutes, then let cool slightly.

Meanwhile, place the fruit kabobs over hot coals and cook for 5 minutes, turning and basting frequently with the melted butter, until the fruit is just tender. Transfer the fruit kabobs to warmed serving plates and serve with the cooled toffee sauce.

serves 4

1 tbsp butter, softened

8 oz/225 g semisweet or milk chocolate

4 large bananas

2 tbsp rum

sour cream, mascarpone cheese, or ice cream, to serve

grated nutmeg, to decorate

chocolate rum bananas

Take four 10-inch/25-cm squares of aluminum foil and brush them with the butter.

Grate the chocolate. Make a careful slit lengthwise in the peel of each banana, and open just wide enough to insert the chocolate. Place the grated chocolate inside the bananas, along their lengths, then close them up.

Wrap each stuffed banana in a square of foil, then barbecue them over hot coals for 5–10 minutes, or until the chocolate has melted inside the bananas. Remove from the barbecue, place the bananas on individual serving plates, and pour some rum into each banana.

Serve immediately with sour cream, mascarpone cheese, or ice cream, topped with nutmeg.

serves 4

4 peaches

6 oz/175 g mascarpone
cheese

1 1/2 oz/40 g pecans or
walnuts, chopped

1 tsp corn oil

4 tbsp maple syrup

mascarpone peaches

Cut the peaches in half and remove the pits. If you are preparing this recipe in advance, press the peach halves together and wrap in plastic wrap until required.

Mix the mascarpone cheese and pecans together in a bowl until well combined. Leave to chill in the refrigerator until required. Preheat the barbecue. Brush the peach halves with a little corn oil and place on a rack set over medium–hot coals. Cook the peach halves for 5–10 minutes, turning once, until hot.

Transfer the peach halves to a serving dish and top with the mascarpone and nut mixture. Drizzle the maple syrup over the top and serve immediately.

serves 4

1 pineapple

3 tbsp dark rum

2 tbsp brown sugar

1 tsp ground ginger

2 oz/55 g unsalted butter, melted

totally tropical pineapple

Preheat the barbecue. Using a sharp knife, cut off the crown of the pineapple, then cut the fruit into 3/4 inch/2 cm thick slices. Cut away the peel from each slice and flick out the "eyes" with the tip of the knife. Stamp out the cores with an apple corer or small cookie cutter.

Mix the rum, sugar, ginger, and butter together in a measuring cup, stirring constantly, until the sugar has dissolved. Brush the pineapple rings with the rum mixture.

Cook the pineapple rings over hot coals for 3–4 minutes on each side. Transfer to serving plates and serve immediately with the remaining rum mixture poured over them.

serves 4

8 fresh figs

scant 1/2 cup cream cheese

1 tsp ground cinnamon

3 tbsp brown sugar

plain yogurt, sour cream, mascarpone cheese, or ice cream, to serve

stuffed figs

Cut out eight 7-inch/18-cm squares of aluminum foil. Make two small slits in each fig, then place each fig on a square of foil.

Put the cream cheese in a bowl. Add the cinnamon and stir until well combined. Stuff the inside of each fig with the cream cheese mixture, then sprinkle a teaspoon of sugar over each one. Close the foil around each fig to make a package.

Place the packages on the barbecue and cook over hot coals, turning them frequently, for about 10 minutes, or until the figs are cooked to your taste.

Transfer the figs to serving plates and serve immediately with plain yogurt, sour cream, mascarpone cheese, or ice cream.

serves 4

8 oz/225 g strawberries

2 tbsp superfine sugar

6 tbsp Marsala wine

$1/2$ tsp ground cinnamon

4 slices panettone

4 tbsp mascarpone cheese

panettone with mascarpone & strawberries

Hull and slice the strawberries and place them in a bowl. Add the sugar, Marsala, and cinnamon to the strawberries.

Toss the strawberries in the sugar and cinnamon mixture until they are well coated. Let chill in the refrigerator for at least 30 minutes. Preheat the barbecue. When ready to serve, transfer the slices of panettone to a rack set over medium–hot coals. Cook the panettone for 1 minute on each side, or until golden brown.

Remove the panettone from the barbecue and transfer to serving plates. Top the panettone with the mascarpone cheese and the marinated strawberries. Serve immediately.

serves 4

2 nectarines, halved and pitted

2 kiwis

4 red plums

1 mango, peeled, halved, and pitted

2 bananas, peeled and thickly sliced

8 strawberries, hulled

1 tbsp honey

3 tbsp Cointreau

mixed fruit kabobs

Cut the nectarine halves into wedges and place in a large, shallow dish. Peel and quarter the kiwis. Cut the plums in half and remove the pits. Cut the mango flesh into chunks and add to the dish with the kiwis, plums, bananas, and strawberries.

Mix the honey and Cointreau together in a measuring cup until blended. Pour the mixture over the fruit and toss to coat. Cover with plastic wrap and let marinate in the refrigerator for 1 hour.

Preheat the barbecue. Drain the fruit, reserving the marinade. Thread the fruit onto several presoaked wooden skewers and cook over medium–hot coals, turning and brushing frequently with the reserved marinade, for 5–7 minutes, then serve.

makes 2 litres

6 cups red grape juice

1¹/₄ cups orange juice

3 measures cranberry juice

2 measures lemon juice

2 measures lime juice

4 measures sugar syrup

ice cubes

to decorate

slices of lemon

slices of orange

slices of lime

soft sangria

Put the grape juice, orange juice, cranberry juice, lemon juice, lime juice, and sugar syrup into a chilled punch bowl and stir well.

Add the ice and decorate with the slices of lemon, orange, and lime.